To my dad, for all he has taught me.

To my whole family, for being there for me.

To Wayne, Dianne, and Andy, without whom our firm could not function.

To all my staff, for their unqualified support.

*And to my clients, for letting Supon Design Group express its talents
and creativity through their projects.*

— Supon Phornirunlit

ISBN 0-945814-33-X

Distributed to the trade throughout the world by
Books Nippan
1123 Dominguez Street, Unit K
Carson, CA 90746
Fax: (310) 604-1134

Published by
SDPress
1717 K Street, NW, Suite 415
Washington, DC 20006

Printed in the United States of America

ACKNOWLEDGMENTS

Creative Director
Supon Phornirunlit

Art Director
Andrew Dolan

Managing Editors
Wayne Kurie
Supon Phornirunlit

Editor
Linda Klinger

Assistant Art Directors
Richard Boynton
Dianne Cook

Photographers
Barry Myers
Oi Veerasarn

Camera Services
Quadrant Slide Services

Desktop Publishing
CompuPrint, Washington, D.C.

Printer
Westland Printers

Papers
Mohawk Recycled 50/10 Gloss,
80 lb Cover and 100 lb Text

Natural, Parchment, Antique White, 80 lb Text

Special thank you's to
Kelly Crossley
Henry Kornman
Laura Shore
Jamie Wynne

INTRODUCTION

IF A DESIGN IS GOOD, SAY THOSE WHO KNOW, IT'S ALSO INTELLIGENT. INTELLIGENT GRAPHICS ARE THOSE that embody thought and appropriateness. The theory has always been popular in the respected corners of the design community, but it's now fast gaining credibility in the corporate world as well. There's a reason why great visuals are produced with a specific look, angle, or proportion. The act of putting reason before reaction is called "smart design." Once a firm becomes established, continued success in the design field means the artwork produced must be appropriate to the project — it must always fit. Although you can have a clever concept without a good solution, you cannot produce great design without intelligence, thought, or method behind it. It may not be familiar or symmetrical or analytical, but it must be reasonable. A product can singularly please the eye but fail to meet the needs or intent of the project. When the piece doesn't pack the punch expected, it's often because the concept simply was not thought through. How do designers conjure up smart design? The objectives of the project should drive the concept which, in turn, should drive the design. If one can infuse style, originality, and a bit of attitude as well, one may well have an award-winning piece. The benefits of smart design are many. We're a visual society: smart design leaves a good first impression. It represents the client with an exclamation point, illustrates a company's ethics and values, or confronts important questions without intimidation. Smart design levels the playing field when a new product or service steps into the marketplace, and may promote an unknown company to the forefront of its league of contenders. It condenses emotion and power into color, line, or placement on a page. Smart design can be simple, but its effect is complex and multi-layered. But, like a documented report or a well-written drama, designers must do their homework and refuse to rush the process. Experimentation is an ongoing process, but it rarely means a fast, smooth leap from the blank page to finished piece without several stalls along the way. Smart design requires a period of research and reflection. The time quota is part of the concept. And a studio called Supon Design Group has based its career on the belief that smart design is the only solution to its visual and marketing challenges.

SUPON DESIGN GROUP

SUPON DESIGN GROUP WAS BORN IN A ONE-BEDROOM APARTMENT IN A QUIET D.C. NEIGHBORHOOD. IN A MANNER that was to become typical of this growth-oriented company, its evolution into its current custom-designed headquarters housing a dozen employees in Washington's major business district was purposeful and quick. In a time period surprisingly short for this type of business, Supon Design Group had established an international reputation among both clients and the design community. ※ The firm has collected 350 awards since opening their doors in July 1988 — Addys, Art Directors Clubs of both Washington and New York, Type Directors Club, and almost every major design recognition in the nation. They've exhibited in England, Germany, Israel, Japan, Thailand, and the U.S., and have been featured in magazines such as *HOW*, AIGA's *Journal*, the Asian publication *Media Delite*, and Germany's *Page* magazine. They've been interviewed on radio and television around the world. Today, recognized, manageable, and still enjoying the process that made it known, Supon Design Group stands at an enviable place in the industry. ※ The key behind Supon Design Group's accomplishments is not a clandestine strategy. It's their determination to serve not just a single group of clients, but a diversity — not-for-profits, public relations firms, corporations, media conglomerates, and small entrepreneurships with only an employee or two — and to serve them intelligently. The company's flexibility and ability to speak the language of many business cultures and values (vital components of smart design) is one of their most critical strengths. ※ Supon Design Group grasps a firm position in the difficult and sometimes temperamental world of business — consistent growth, project variety, customer loyalty, and public recognition keep Supon Design Group's name out in front. In the speculative arena of simple economics, this studio has proven itself to be an able contender. Supon Design Group is currently comprised of three segments: its original Graphic Design division, the very successful International Book Division, and a brand-new division devoted to product design. The company sees such diversification as vital to both its short- and long-term growth strategies. Samples of work from each of these areas are featured in the "Portfolio" section of this book.

PHILOSOPHY

SUPON DESIGN GROUP ARRIVED IN THE INDUSTRY — AS DO SO MANY NEW COMPANIES — WITH ITS VISION angled wide and its goals pointed toward the stars. It entered with its best foot forward and quickly established itself as a unique design organization, both from within and without. Its management did not confine itself to trademark art, or print design, or computer-generated solutions; they filled the studio with books and toys, pencils and crayons and diskettes, and they don't seem to have stopped exploring yet. Their graphics were directed, thoughtful, and consistently communicative. Design started with ideas, matured through production, and realized itself through the color, the texture, the curve of a letterform, and the angle of a paper fold. 🐜 Today, the company is made up of talented individuals with complementary approaches and artistic styles. With contrasting backgrounds, each person has a slightly different perspective on projects, resulting in a good mix of viewpoints, experience, and goals. Correspondingly, clients seem to share in the kinship that the company worked hard to build. Clients who were drawn to the studio by its reputation or by recommendation stay loyal, they say, because the staff makes them feel welcome and confident that Supon Design Group will portray them appropriately. A few local clients actually prefer to stop by the studio when a fax or phone call would have sufficed, just to say hello. One or two will admit to coming by just to play with the company mascot, Pica, a miniature Pomeranian. 🐜 Supon Design Group has also established a rapport with design industry professionals because of their mutual respect and shared interests. In the design field, there is always more to learn. Supon Design Group's association with industry organizations and willingness to speak at conferences afford the staff the opportunity not only to keep updated in current techniques, but also to give something back to the design community. But Supon Design Grouphas always maintained a perspective of "business first." They service repeat clients and win new ones by adhering to a strict sense of propriety and professionalism. At Supon Design Group, that simple tenet has kept their name solid and reputable within its industry.

SELF-PROMOTION

DESIGN FIRMS ROUTINELY PROMOTE THEMSELVES, DEFINING THEIR OWN IMAGE IN THE MARKETPLACE AND attracting clients who identify with that impression. Self-promotion is a necessary part of a studio's marketing efforts, providing occasions to demonstrate scope and breadth, and at times ensuring their survival during periods of economic downturns or slow seasons. The visual splendor of exceptional design is widely lauded by both professional and lay audiences, but it's not the only feature of a superior studio promotion. What makes the difference is that characteristic called good marketing. And part of a careful marketing strategy is illustrating how exciting and effective a good visual can be to the bottom line of the right audience. Although the frequency of studio self-promotion efforts is acknowledged, the direction it takes varies greatly. Supon Design Group has a plethora of approaches that speak to a variety of markets. One example is their brochure "Design That Makes A Statement" — an elegant, conservative piece that addresses the professional relationship between clients and vendors. With its magnificent photos, spare text, and subtle colors, it targets corporations and firms considered to be traditional. The promotional package "Spellbound," on the other hand, is more jaunty, using wit, full color, and additional pages to make its point. "Spellbound" was the first promotion to actually display Supon Design Group's work, and it did so playfully, involving its audience directly in the company sensibility. It found a ready audience in television and radio stations, restaurants, and technology firms. Studios disagree as much about the cost of promoting themselves as they do about how to go about it. Some insist that profits should go into computer upgrades or an impressive office address. At Supon Design Group, the general philosophy is that 20 percent or more of each year's profits go into the next year's self-promotions. "You have to spend money to make money," says principal Supon Phornirunlit. Money spent on self-promotion, he believes, is an investment in one's business and one's future. From all indications, he may indeed be right.

The "S" in Supon Design Group's logo was die-cut to reveal the yellow flysheet in this dramatic, first use of the company's current identity. Fittingly, the booklet is a compilation of corporate identities done for a variety of clients.

"Spellbound" reflects Supon Design Group's playfulness. Hidden inside a magic-hat box are a full-color portfolio booklet and a T-shirt featuring one of the three icons at right. Each piece announces that, like magic, Supon Design Group has found the secret to good design.

Far right: An elegantly conservative promotion, "Design That Makes A Statement" addresses the business relationship between clients and vendors. Its spare text and magnificent photography target corporations and more traditional firms.

OUR REPUTATION PRECEDES US.

Supon Design Group has established itself as a sound, dependable studio in the Washington area. We work with our clients to give their project a personal touch. We've kept the size of the company small, and recruited some of the brightest talent in the area. Our many graphics awards attest to our achievement in the industry. But our reputation, built through the consistent satisfaction of our customers, remains our proudest accomplishment.

AS WITH MAGIC, THERE'S A SECRET TO GOOD DESIGN.

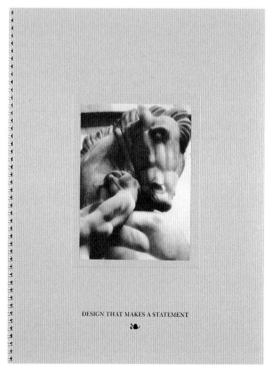

DESIGN THAT MAKES A STATEMENT

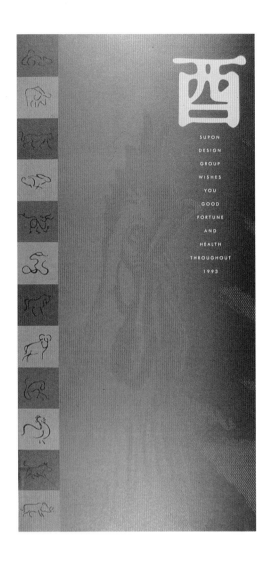

Varied design styles are apparent in these four different "give-aways" to clients, vendors, and designers. Chinese New Year poster, T-shirt commemorating a speaking engagement, and notepads. Opposite: Holiday stationery

AWARDS

THE IMPACT OF AWARDS ON BOTH THE STUDIO AND ITS CLIENTS IS MUCH GREATER THAN THE arrangement of plaques or sculptures that hang on a wall or sit on ashelf. Awards are your peers' attempt to recognize the great from the good, to separate the self-conscious from the inspired. For clients, even one design award can mean verification of the skill and talent of the designers in whom they've placed their trust. Awards are one way to build relations with clients. A studio earns respectability when customers see their own projects cited on a list of award-winners, and they feel more confident contracting the services of a designer who has brought them notoriety. For the studio, recognition by its colleagues is the highest form of tribute — a nod from those who recognize greatness in the industry. Honors are important barometers for designers who continue to grow and refine their talents and skills, and awards ensure they're on the right track. Supon Design Group has received enough awards to convince the most cynical of its design suitability and creative prowess. Today, the firm enters competitions selectively — only the most critical and respected. Their winning entries, which are then frequently published in prestigious anthologies and magazines, extend the firm's reach further, and their reputation, wider. Awards certainly are not the goal of smart design, but a smart designer recognizes their value in both pride and public relations.

PORTFOLIO

SUPON DESIGN GROUP'S EXPE-RIENCE SPANS THE SPECTRUM. AND THAT'S WHAT THE STAFF likes most. "One day, we may be working on a very technical scientific journal where every dot and dash has meaning; the next, it'll be a fanciful identity where the sky's the limit, or product packaging with its own mandates." Every project is different. Each has its own history, objectives, restrictions, and possibilities — and all is dependent on the audience and the problem to be solved. Supon Design Group's clientele is diverse and its portfolio reflects this fact. On any given day, the studio may have as many as 50-60 projects in production. Some may take but a week, from start to finish; others go through refinements or evolutions that may take six months or more. Budgets range too, from low-paying projects for not-for-profit fundraising, to full-throttle corporate identities for which high dollar is paid. But whatever the project, the quality is the same. At times, this may be difficult to maintain and even harder to define. But it's not hard to recognize. Supon Design Group has met the challenge of producing products of consistent quality. They say that they get their inspiration from everything — from art to science — but it's apparent that their style and attention to detail comes from their willingness to stay open-minded and focused — and to be original when justified. It also helps when the staff truly enjoys what they're doing. The company's sense of image and fun can best be demonstrated by its work. Just look at the range of ideas that could never originate from a stagnant mind, or one dulled by routine or a closed environment. On the following pages are 80 projects. Not many, but representative of the thousands done by Supon and his staff over the past five years.

GreenCity
MARKET & CAFE

GreenCity
MARKET & CAFE

4735 BETHESDA AVENUE, BETHESDA, MARYLAND 20814

GreenCity's Market and Café stocks only fresh, natural foods. Its identity, therefore, was designed with an upscale, health-conscious clientele in mind.

Clockwise from upper left:
Louise Owen III, watchmaker.
Robinson Radiology, radiologist.
Charles Button Company,
  button manufacturer.
Ulman Paper Bag Company,
  bag manufacturer.
Center: Bugs and Bees, toy stores.

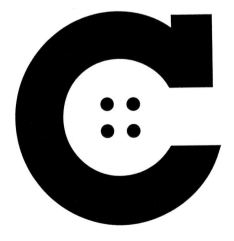

Variations on Discovery
Communications' existing logo
for its three new divisions.

**PRODUCTIONS
WORLDWIDE**

ENTERPRISES

INTERNATIONAL

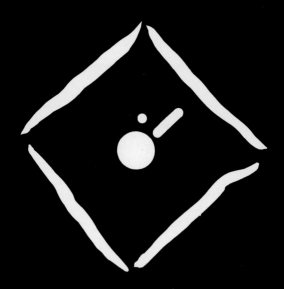

Three high-tech logos. From top:
Vertical Marketing, Inc.,
    Software Development.
Telocator: The Personal
    Communications Association.
The U.S. Postal Forum.

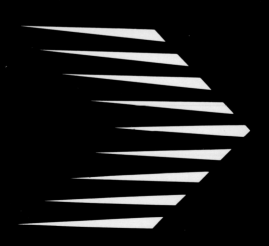

The identity for the Art Directors Club of Metropolitan Washington had to be both innovative and inexpensive to produce. With black-and-white photos subjected to several generations of photocopying to produce a distressed look, this system fit the bill.

Environ-Mentality is a campaign
which promotes ecological
awareness on college campuses.
Its graphic look and concerned
message appeal to today's students.

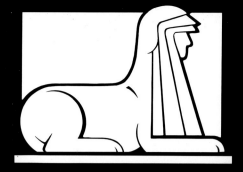

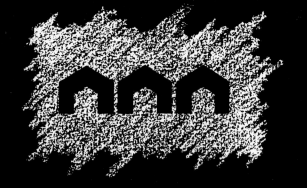

Clockwise from upper left:
Dupont Circle Citizens Association.
Low-Income Housing Conference.
Environ-Mentality.
Kids and AIDS.
Center: Membership Campaign for
    YMCA of Metropolitan Washington.

Clothing tags for Bangkok's
Byzantine stores and Dallas' Planet
Called Earth, both targeting the
young, sophisticated, and urbane.

An image of gentleness is portrayed by the sweetly drawn identity for V/S Spa and Massage Club in Thailand. Earlier sketches below.

Diverse Handle and Giggle are both gift shops which sell a wide array of trendy, offbeat wares. Although their solutions are quite dissimilar, their objectives are the same.

For added visual interest, the product tags for X International display variations on the store's basic identity.

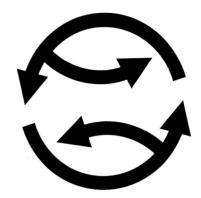

Clockwise, from upper left:
National Institute for the
   Conservation of Cultural Property.
"How-to" Tennis Clinic for
   underprivileged kids.
Thomas Radcliffe Mignerey,
   copywriter.
The Cat's Meow, progressive clothing
   store for women.
Center: Queen of Fashion,
   vintage clothing store.

Opposite: Circle Boy Classic is a line
of clothing which targets the young
male, 18-35, with updates on old-
time favorites. A Roman column,
rendered in trendy colors and
graphics, presents this image to
the consumer.

APPETIZERS

ASIANA GRILLED TOFU   3.95
Grilled fresh tofu with light soy bean sauce.

SATE ON SKEWERS   4.95
Grilled marinated beef on skewers splashed with peanut curry sauce.

CRYING TIGER   6.95
Grilled steak served with tearfully spicy tamarind dipping sauce.

YUMMY SEAFOOD   6.95
Fresh seafood and glass noodles marinated with herbs in spicy lime juice.

ZESTY CRAB   6.95
Fresh crab meat seasoned in spicy lime juice with fresh cilantro.

SKEWER SQUID   4.95
Grilled sliced fresh squid with lightly spicy sweet & sour chili sauce.

ASIANA ROLLS   4.95
Wrapped crab stick, tofu, cucumber, and egg served with plum sauce.

CRISPY TOFU   3.95
Deep fried tofu with lightly spicy sweet & sour sauce.

LUCKY CHICKEN CUP   4.95
Chopped grilled chicken marinated with spicy fresh herbs in lettuce cup.

EAST WEST SHRIMP   6.95
Shrimp wrapped with bacon fried crispy served with house's B.B.Q sauce.

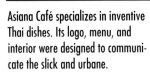

Asiana Café specializes in inventive
Thai dishes. Its logo, menu, and
interior were designed to communi-
cate the slick and urbane.

Starters

Ravioli and Oyster Tartare	8.75
io, Sesame Seed and Roast Bell Pepper Relish	7.75
on in Potato Crust, Citrus Dill Vinaigrette	9.00
I Shiitake in Lobster Basil Cream	8.75
Ovendried Tomatoes and Roast Corn	9.75
h Lentil Relish, Cider Vinegar Dressing	8.25

Soups

Aioli Croutons and California Beans	10.00
with Spinach Shiitake Ravioli and Quail Egg	6.00

Salads

h Baked Goat Cheese in Phyllo	7.00
I in Hazelnut Vinaigrette	5.75
d with Pears and Walnut Dressing	8.80

Main Courses

dfish, Spinach Puree, Horseradish Chive Sabayon	23.50
Asparagus, Capellini, Late Harvest Riesling Cream	31.00
Breast, Orange Merlot Sauce, Basmati Rice	26.00
mb with Mild Goat Cheese and Almond Crust, Saffron Jus	29.5
Gras and Madeira Port Sauce	27.50
s, Carmelized Granny Smith Apples	34.50
Rice Paper Crust, Lobster Ginger Essence	23.00

Desserts

	6.00
	7.50
	7.50

Le Café de la Mauvaise Cuisine aims for a very hip and progressive clientele — one which can look past the restaurant's tongue-in-cheek name.

Uchman, Ltd. distributes specialty
papers by direct mail. The final
identity suggests the featherweight
characteristic of paper. Earlier
sketches at bottom.

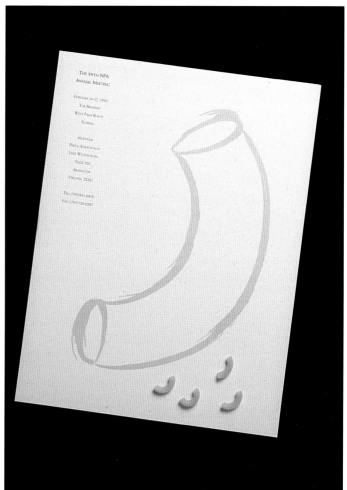

Stationery showing the whimsical
identity of National Pasta
Association's 89th Annual Meeting.

The packaging for Adonis Spring
Water was designed to appeal to
upscale Westerners traveling in Asia.
The delicate, virginal figure suggests
the freshness and purity of the
water.

Its taste altered to appeal to the Asian palate, Naturally Spaghetti Sauce still retains its homestyle identity. The label's illustration of a peasant hard at work reinforces this message.

CD packaging for Julie Budd, Dead Girlfriend, and Berserk. The design of each is a function of the artist's musical style and image.
(Julie Budd, Bernstein Enterprises; Berserk, Go-Kart Records.)

Carrier box and written communication strategy for World Cup Soccer's 1994 dossier. The spiral-bound booklet features a bold and imaginative cover, suggestive of the creative approach that Supon Design Group would bring to the project.

15TH

15

T DESIGNERS' ASSOCIATION
UAL GOLD AND SILVER AWARDS

3 BDA Gold and Silver Award
st television and video design
DA is honored to publish this
creators, not only for their
dedication to their craft.

GES

Robin Stelling
Jill Taffet
Kathy Thaden
Christopher Wargin
Ron Willis

aria LoConte

lication
an

1993

FIFTEENTH ANNUAL GOLD AND SILVER AWARDS

B D A

BROADCAST DESIGNERS' ASSOCIATION

IATION

4107 | 415.543.6330

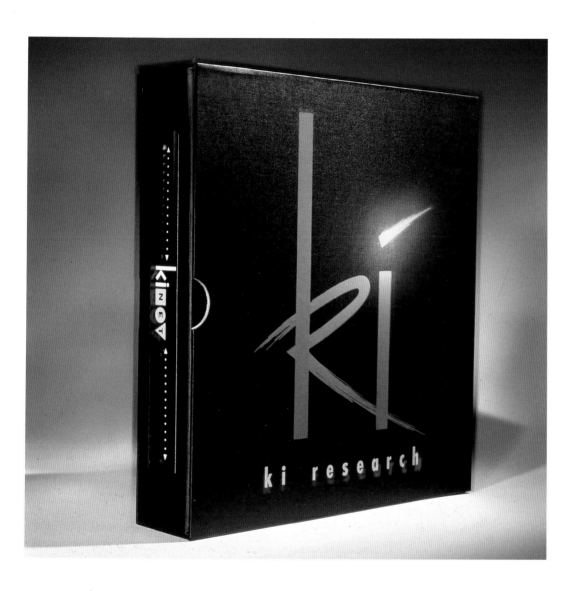

ki research

ki Research is the developer of kinet, a line of connectivity software. Since its name is derived from *ki*, the Japanese word for "tree," a high-tech swash, suggestive of Asian calligraphy, is used in its identity. Earlier sketches at bottom.

Opposite: The artistic identity for the 15th Annual Awards Competition of the Broadcast Designers' Association is shown here on videotape packaging. The look is bold and multi-layered, suggestive of today's many different media options.

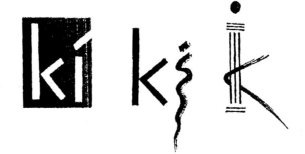

The identity for the first competition of International Self-Promotion suggests its world-wide reach.

Right: The theme of this year's event by the Art Directors Club of Metropolitan Washington was "American Originals," captured on the cover and throughout the booklet by icons such as Elvis Presley, the space shuttle, and the light bulb.

Cover and interior spread of the members list for the Art Directors Club of Metropolitan Washington. The posterization of photos of Washington landmarks (The Jefferson Memorial, above, and National Cathedral, below) continues a practice launched with the organization's identity (page 23).

INTRODUCTION

The Art Directors Club of Metropolitan Washington (ADCMW) is a not-for-profit organization of more than 500 creators, supervisors, producers and students of graphic design, photography and illustration and individuals from allied fields that support these efforts.

The club was formed in 1953 to advance the quality of service and the standards of integrity, honor and courtesy among those actively engaged in the field of graphic design; to foster a fraternal spirit among the members; to promote a code of professional ethics and rules of conduct that encourages and promotes honest and fair dealings between art directors and clients, associates, government and the general public; to offer guidance and promote the welfare of students planning to enter the profession; and to sponsor educational and social activities for the members.

The club implements these goals by offering programs on important graphic design issues for the members and the general public throughout the year; by presenting lectures, meeting, and social events specifically for members during the year; by sponsoring competitions and programs for graphic design students in the region; and by producing and enforcing a Code of Fair Practices.

Frank Parsons Paper Company sells dozens of different coated papers in all price and quality ranges. Because donuts are often coated and come in many colors and flavors, they were chosen as the theme for a first-ever comparison kit. Samples of each sheet offered are inside, each printed with a halftone, duotone, full color, and gloss and dull varnishes. Sketches at bottom depict earlier concepts of "coated."

Opposite: The publications catalog and membership brochure of The Society of Industrial and Office Realtors both contain watercolor art of architectural elements such as columns, pediments, windows, and gables. The velvety images rendered on uncoated paper create the impression of texture and depth.

Shape The Vision

THE PARTNERSHIP FOR RECYCLING
NATIONAL RECYCLING COALITION

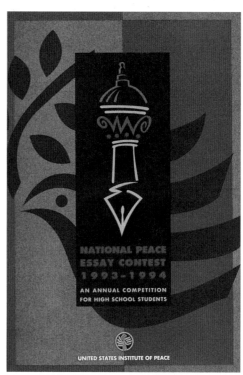

NATIONAL PEACE
ESSAY CONTEST
1993-1994
AN ANNUAL COMPETITION
FOR HIGH SCHOOL STUDENTS

UNITED STATES INSTITUTE OF PEACE

Strong colors and bold graphics
unite these three very different
pieces: Shape the Vision, a
promotional brochure for the
National Recycling Coalition; a
brochure for an essay contest
sponsored by the United States
Institute of Peace; and an operating
survey for the National Wholesale
Druggists' Association.

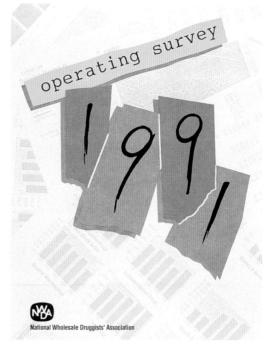

operating survey

1991

National Wholesale Druggists' Association

The Interactive Library are educational videodiscs and printed manuals produced by Discovery Communications for use in the classroom. The marketing package shown here consists of a carrier summarizing the product's benefits and six different inserts, one for each volume.

BUILDING
AN
IMAGE

SOUTHERN PRINTING COMPANY

Southern Printing Company's objective was to break into the Washington, D.C. design market. With over a dozen different inks and printing techniques plus dramatic photography of capital-area landmarks, this brochure speaks to its audience.

You respond to your customers' needs with print materials of the highest criterion, produced by professionals with an exceptional reputation. What makes a business distinctive is skills that evolve with experience, attention to detail—and the inevitable hard work. At Southern Printing, building an image also means building your confidence in our organization. We appreciate your trust, and work to keep it, one client at a time.

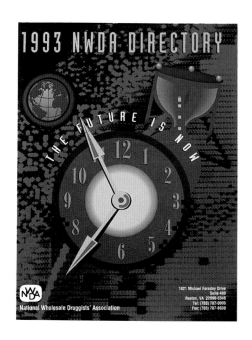

Whether futuristic, graphic, or emotional, a dramatic illustration style is always effective.
Left to right: Member directory, National Wholesale Druggists' Association;
Product marketing brochure, Pritech;
Artistic Freedom Under Attack, People For the American Way.

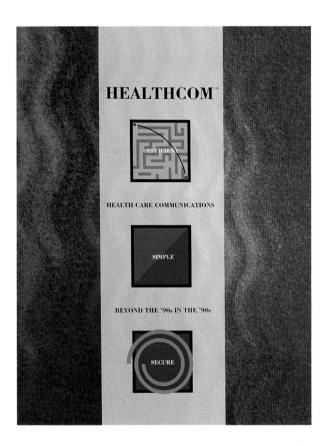

A brochure describing the benefits of Healthcom, an electronic network of healthcare members, conveys both the economic and technological benefits of the system.

HEALTHCOM™'s

advantage starts with its creation. By bringing together members of the health care distribution community to create a communications resource that meets their individual and collective needs, HEALTHCOM™ delivers what it promises: a whole new era of operational efficiency and effectiveness.

At its core is a communications-based database that allows users who already have entered information to share it with others who have similar needs. This way, information is entered once, accurate and available immediately. By consolidating data entry into a single, shared electronic data interchange network, costs are significantly reduced and errors virtually eliminated. Moreover, with everyone sharing in maintaining the system, all users receive the benefits of the newest technologies and applications without having to shoulder the burden of covering the entire cost alone.

HEALTHCOM™ is a users'network. You determine what you want and how it will work through an Application Steering Committee. Members define what goes on the network, the priority of new application development, document standards, security requirements and billing methods.

With HEALTHCOM™, industry trading partners profit from a communications network dedicated to serving their needs, not someone else's bottom line.

THE DATABASE

The communications database would offer more information than industry members currently receive. Plus it would be faster, more accurate and cheaper to both change information and receive it. Opportunities exist to share information on:

- Product specifications
- Specialized pricing
- Transportation/ materials handling
- Special promotion details

BIG SAVINGS

An industry-sponsored study revealed that wholesalers and manufacturers could save between $550 million and $900 million by establishing a lower cost electronic data interchange network and using it for standard business transactions. Gone would be duplicate data entry, clerical errors and multiple charges for transmitting the same information. In its place would be:

- improved price and promotion management;
- better inventory management;
- lower communications costs;
- error-free data; and
- reduced clerical costs.

The key to achieving these savings is a commitment to using electronic communications via HEALTHCOM™ so its volume share grows rapidly.

If You Think
Unions
are only
Interested
in
Wages
and
Benefits

THINK
AGAIN

To reverse its public image, the AFL-CIO wanted a brochure which would convey the community services provided by unions.

"We hid in the bathroom. We could hear the roofs caving in one by one, getting closer to us, then the roofs on both sides of us went and ours was the only one standing."

—Terry Jarrett
United Paperworkers
International Union

Disaster Relief

When Hurricane Andrew roared through South Florida, homes and lives were destroyed in an instant. For Terry Jarrett, it seemed that things couldn't get worse. After having worked for ten years at a cement plant in Homestead, Florida, he had recently been diagnosed with leukemia and forced to quit his job.

After the winds died down, it was Jarrett's union that came through for him and his wife, Carolyn, offering emergency cash relief and perhaps most importantly, a quick path through red tape to secure emergency housing for Jarrett and his wife. "The union made sure we got a washer and dryer and a fan and other things I needed."

"We had help - money, supplies, volunteer workers - coming in from unions all over" says Bill Bowen, president of the Papermakers local in Homestead, Florida.

Union halls served as the headquarters for Red Cross Disaster Services and as information and referral centers. Hundreds of AFL-CIO Building Trades Council volunteers repaired homes, members of the local teachers' union bought school supplies for children living in tent cities and unions from across the country donated relief supplies and set up food banks.

And the work went on. Months later, union members and community services representatives were still on the scene, working every day to rebuild the community and restore hope.

Keith Haring
Untitled

John Evans, Sibley/Peteet Graphic Design
Untitled

OVERVIEW

The NCAP model of enabling com
develop strategies for addressing
relies on the strong "partnership"
last four years among NCAP, the Local P
grantees. The model's success lies in the
strategic nature of local grantmaking pro
Each community's mix of grants is u
are common threads running throughout
projects — from an interdisciplinary ca
community, to a statewide policy initia
tion program for incarcerated youth —
strategies that are "risky" or unproven.
culturally sensitive and appropriate are
sites, as are interventions targeting har
populations.
This past year the original Senior
their four year tenure in the challeng
With some grants still scheduled to b
fifth year, their cumulative total now
$17,864,290 in grants made to 709 g
the Associate Partners made 167 gra
$1,649,485, as of June 30, 1992.

NATIONAL COMMUNITY AIDS PARTNERSHIP

1991-1992 ANNUAL REPORT

The innocence of the fifties is brought back by this calendar for the American Association of Retired Persons' Legal Council for the Elderly. Retro colors, graphics, and photos make it a nostalgic trip back through time.

Left: The annual report of the National Community AIDS Partnership was printed in an economical two colors. Before binding, however, full-color donated artwork was inserted as divider pages throughout the publication. Such creative thinking and community generosity made a full-color report possible for this non-profit organization.

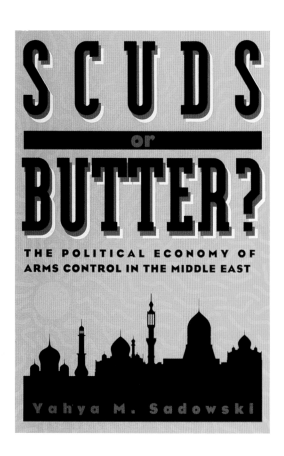

SCUDS
or
BUTTER?

THE POLITICAL ECONOMY OF
ARMS CONTROL IN THE MIDDLE EAST

Yahya M. Sadowski

WHO BEARS
THE LIFETIME
TAX BURDEN?

DON FULLERTON *and* DIANE LIM ROGERS

A TWENTIETH CENTURY FUND BOOK
Rights at
WORK

EMPLOYMENT RELATIONS IN THE POST-UNION ERA

RICHARD EDWARDS

BRIDGING
THE
GAP

Theory & Practice
In Foreign Policy

ALEXANDER L. GEORGE

DISCOVER JAPAN

All Nippon Airways 1993 Summer Program in Japan

An adventure of a lifetime awaits you. Five DC area students will be chosen to spend the summer of '94 with Japanese host families. Contact your guidance counselor today for an application or Youth for Understanding at 202-673-2728. Students must have a C average or better and demonstrate general suitability for a cross-cultural living experience. The ANA Summer Program in Japan is administered by YFU International exchange.

ANA
All Nippon Airways
Japan's best to the world.

"Discover Japan" is All Nippon Airways' cross-cultural exchange program for American students. The artwork links today's air travel with Japan's traditional art of origami. An earlier concept is shown below.

Opposite: Dramatic typography combines with illustrations in each of these book covers: *Scuds or Butter?*, Brookings Institution; *Who Bears the Lifetime Tax Burden?*, Brookings Institution; *Rights at Work*, Brookings Institution; *Bridging the Gap*, United States Institute of Peace.

MODERN |ART|

THE ROBERT G. ANDERSON
GALLERY INVITES YOU TO AT-
TEND THE GALA OPENING OF
ITS EXHIBITION BY VARIETY OF
ARTISTS, ENTITLED " MODERN
ART IN THE 80'S," ON JANUARY
15, 1991. OPENING RECEPTION:
6:00 PM - 9:00 PM. EXHIBITION
ON VIEW THROUGH JANUARY
31,1991.

MODERN |ART|

THE ROBERT G. ANDERSON
GALLERY INVITES YOU TO AT-
TEND THE GALA OPENING OF
ITS EXHIBITION BY VARIETY OF
ARTISTS, ENTITLED " MODERN
ART IN THE 80'S," ON JANUARY
15, 1991. OPENING RECEPTION:
6:00 PM - 9:00 PM. EXHIBITION
ON VIEW THROUGH JANUARY
31,1991.

Printed in black only on granite-like
grey paper, these posters for the
opening of a modern art exhibition
were very economical to produce.

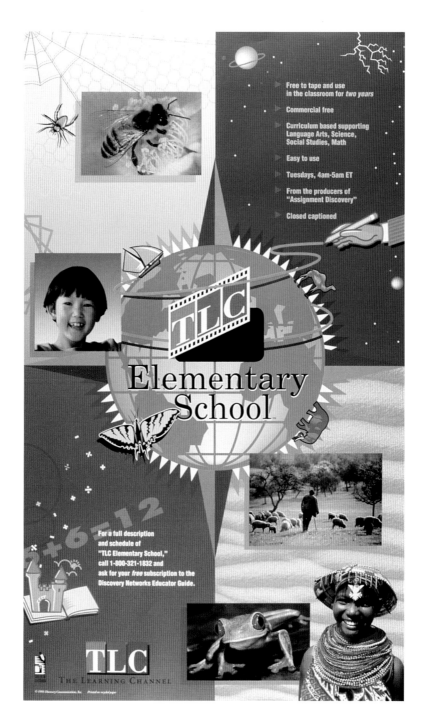

"TLC Elementary School" is an educational program on The Learning Channel. Its promotional poster suggests the world of possibilities available to those who learn.

SUPON DESIGN GROUP'S PRODUCT DIVISION

With the debut of "Iconopolis®" in 1993, Supon Design Group's commercial product division was born. A computer disk and educational booklet in one, Iconopolis allows graphic designers to use editable EPS icons to enhance their work. Two disks contain a total of 50 city-related icons, from the specific: the Eiffel Tower, the Statue of Liberty, and the White House; to the general: a row of townhouses, a traffic light, and a park bench. A gallery of original art demonstrates how easily color, line width, and size can be altered and how various icons can be combined to create even more possibilities.

A second volume of Iconopolis icons entitled "Our Living Planet" is currently in production. Other upcoming projects include a line of papers and a series of children's playtoys.

SUPON DESIGN GROUP'S INTERNATIONAL BOOK DIVISION

An affiliate of Supon Design Group, the International Book Division has written and designed a total of ten books on graphic design since its founding in 1989. Its purpose: to produce exceptional, well-designed books with interesting and educational content. As graphic designers foremost, Supon Design Group knew what it wanted in design publications. It reviewed what existed, and committed itself to do better — determined to put its own vision to paper. The results? Supon Design Group's very first effort, *International Logos & Trademarks*, sold out within three months, and, since, numerous organizations have honored the books with awards for design and content. And several of Supon Design Group's publications have been featured by book clubs among their main selections.

International Logos & Trademarks, Madison Square Press, 1990

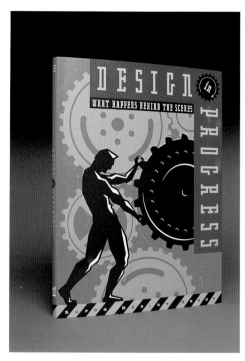

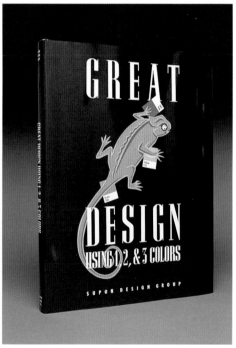

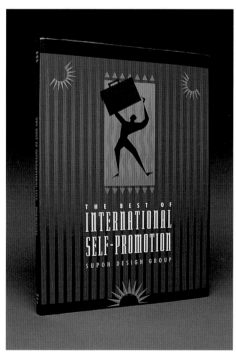

Design in Progress: What Happens Behind the Scenes, Books Nippan, 1992
Great Design Using 1, 2, and 3 Colors, Madison Square Press, 1992
The Best of International Self-Promotion, Madison Square Press, 1993

Successful Logos Worldwide, Books Nippan, 1992
Computer Generation: How Designers View Today's Technology, Books Nippan, 1993
Graphically Bold, Books Nippan, 1993

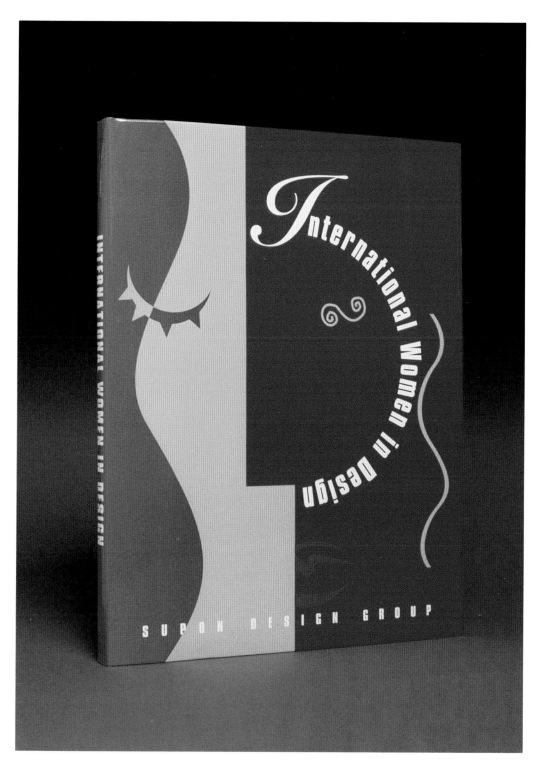

International Women in Design, Madison Square Press, 1993

This publication has been made possible with the generous support of:

Frank Parsons Paper Company, Inc.

2270 Beaver Road

Landover, Maryland 20785